AI Mistakes That Could Cost You Everything

Avoid the Critical Errors That Put Your Business, Data, and Reputation at Risk

Written by
Eric LeBouthillier

AcraSolution | 2025 1st Edition
www.acrasolution.com

Preface

The AI revolution isn't coming — it's already here.
From small businesses to billion-dollar enterprises, organizations everywhere are integrating AI into their workflows, content, strategy, and support. The tools are fast, powerful, and shockingly accessible. But so are the risks.

Over the past year, I've watched smart companies fall victim to AI hallucinations, data leaks, flawed automation, and biased decision-making — not because they were reckless, but because they didn't know where the real dangers were hiding.

The truth is, most AI disasters aren't caused by rogue machines or futuristic threats.
They're caused by **normal people** — using **smart tools** in **untrained environments**.

This book is your field guide to **avoiding those disasters**.

Inside, I'll walk you through the 10 most dangerous and expensive AI mistakes I've seen in real businesses — and more importantly, how to prevent them with smart, clear, and ethical practices.

You don't need to be a developer, data scientist, or AI engineer to read this book.
You just need to care about your company, your data, your team, and your reputation.

Let's get started — before one of these mistakes costs you everything.

— *Eric LeBouthillier*
Author & Cybersecurity Strategist

LEGAL DISCLAIMER

This eBook is provided for informational purposes only and does not constitute legal, financial, or professional advice. The author and publisher have made every reasonable effort to ensure the accuracy and completeness of the information contained herein; however, neither assumes any responsibility for errors, omissions, or contrary interpretations of the subject matter.

Readers are encouraged to consult with qualified professionals for specific advice tailored to their individual needs. The mention of any products, services, or third-party entities does not imply an endorsement or guarantee of their effectiveness or suitability. Any application of the strategies and recommendations presented is at the reader's discretion and risk.

The author and publisher shall not be liable for any damages (including, without limitation, direct, indirect, incidental, or consequential) caused by the use, misuse, or interpretation of the information herein. All references to regulatory standards, statutes, or compliance requirements are informational and do not replace official legal counsel.

By reading and applying the concepts in this eBook, you acknowledge that you bear sole responsibility for the outcomes of your decisions and actions. If you do not agree to these terms, please discontinue use of this publication immediately.

Table of Contents

CHAPTER 8: OVER-RELYING ON CHATBOTS OR AI FOR CUSTOMER SUPPORT   60

CHAPTER 9: ASSUMING YOUR AI VENDOR IS FULLY SECURE   68

CHAPTER 10: NO RECOVERY PLAN FOR AI ERRORS   75

Who This Book Is For

This book is written for anyone responsible for decisions, systems, or people in an organization using — or planning to use — AI tools. You don't need a technical background. You need clarity, control, and risk awareness.

Specifically:

- **Business owners and SMB leaders** using AI to cut costs, write content, or make decisions

- **Consultants, freelancers, and marketers** using tools like ChatGPT, Claude, Bard, or Copilot

- **HR, legal, or compliance professionals** worried about privacy, bias, or data handling

- **IT managers and team leads** looking to implement AI safely across teams

- **Startup founders** integrating AI into their products or business ops

- **Anyone tempted to paste sensitive information into a chatbot without thinking twice**

If your work touches customer data, business strategy, client communication, or internal tools — this book was written for you.

Chapter 1: Trusting AI Without Guardrails

Introduction

Artificial Intelligence is not the future — it's already here, quietly making decisions across your business. From automated financial reporting to customer service, AI tools now influence real-world outcomes at a scale few SMBs truly grasp. But here's the danger: many leaders are relying on AI as if it's a flawless expert. It's not. Believing AI is always right — or even usually right — is a fast path to reputational damage, financial loss, and legal exposure.

This chapter is about one of the most dangerous assumptions in modern business: trusting AI output without question. If you're a business owner or IT lead leaning on AI tools to save time or boost productivity, this is where your guard needs to go *up*, not down.

Let's break down when AI is a reliable assistant — and when it becomes a costly liability.

What AI Is Good At — and What It Should Never Replace

AI is excellent at processing large volumes of data, finding patterns, and performing repetitive tasks at speed. It's like a tireless intern with a photographic memory — but zero judgment.

Where AI Excels:

- **Summarizing** large datasets, emails, or reports
- **Automating** repetitive tasks like scheduling or tagging
- **Generating drafts** of routine content (emails, product descriptions, etc.)
- **Predicting patterns** based on historical data, such as customer behavior or inventory needs

These tasks are time-consuming for humans and pose low risk if slightly off. AI thrives here.

Where AI Fails — And Why You Should Never Let It Lead:

- **Legal interpretation or contract drafting**
- **Financial forecasting or compliance reporting**
- **Medical or ethical decision-making**
- **Customer-facing responses in sensitive scenarios**

In each of these, precision matters. One wrong word, one false assumption, and your business could face legal exposure, financial penalties, or customer backlash. AI lacks common sense, empathy, and legal accountability. It will sound confident — even when it's dead wrong.

AI STRENGTHS	AI NO-GO ZONES
• Data analysis	• Strategic planning
• Process automation	• Creative work
• Forecasting	• Relationship building
• Customer support	• Sensitive decisions
• Sales optimization	• Complex problem-solving

Real-World Case: The AI-Generated Financial Report That Backfired

What Happened:

A mid-sized consultancy deployed an AI tool to auto-generate financial summaries for quarterly board reporting. The tool was trained on historical data and used natural language generation to produce the draft reports. No human analyst was assigned to review the results before distribution.

One quarter, the AI misinterpreted a deferred revenue entry as earned income. It overstated earnings by 18%, which triggered an early bonus payout to executives and a wave of investor confidence.

Unfortunately, the truth emerged during an external audit. The misclassification violated financial reporting standards and exposed the company to legal liability under their investment disclosure obligations.

What Went Wrong:

- **No human-in-the-loop validation**
- **Assumption that AI understood accounting logic**
- **No internal disclaimers or review checkpoints before distribution**

What We Learn:

Even well-trained AI lacks domain understanding. It doesn't "know" accounting — it patterns text that looks like accounting. Without oversight, the results can be dangerously plausible and disastrously wrong.

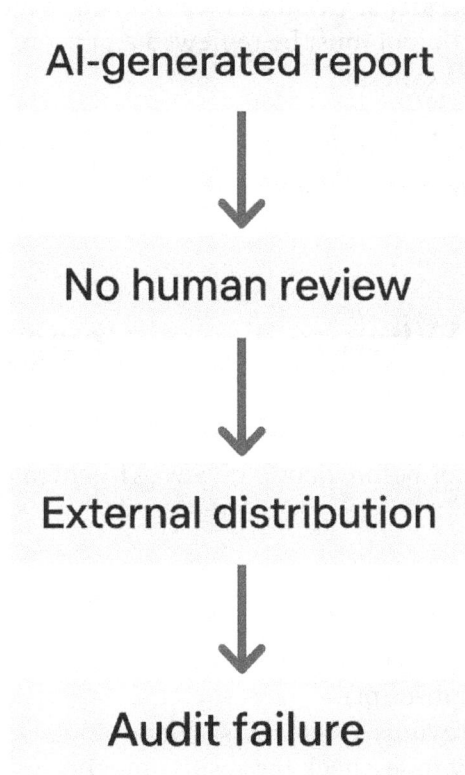

AI-generated report

↓

No human review

↓

External distribution

↓

Audit failure

Tactical Fixes: Making AI Safe to Use in Your Workflow

The good news? You *can* safely use AI — with the right safeguards.

Tactical Best Practices:

- **Human-in-the-loop:** Always require review and approval by a qualified human before AI output goes public or is used in high-impact decisions.
- **Disclaimers:** Clearly label AI-generated content internally, so teams understand it's a draft or suggestion — not a verified source.
- **Validation steps:** Build checkpoints into your workflow where AI output must be reviewed against regulatory, legal, or business criteria.

These steps may feel like slowing down the process. In reality, they're preventing costly cleanup later.

Checklist: When to Trust, Review, or Reject AI Output

Use this quick filter before acting on any AI-generated content in your business:

☑ **Trust** AI output when:

- The task is low-risk and repetitive (e.g., summarizing a meeting transcript)
- You've previously verified similar outputs
- You can double-check the result quickly

🔍 **Review** AI output when:

- The content informs business decisions (e.g., pricing suggestions, strategic drafts)
- It involves customer-facing language
- It includes data that must be accurate (numbers, names, dates)

✖ **Reject** AI output when:

- It includes legal, financial, or contractual claims
- It's unclear how the AI reached its conclusion
- You'd be liable for an error caused by the content

Trust	Review	Reject
Grammar correction	Sales report	Candidate decision
Grammar correction		

Conclusion

AI can be a powerful tool — or a silent threat. Trusting AI without guardrails is not a shortcut; it's a gamble. Your business doesn't need to fear AI, but it does need to *understand it*. Without human oversight, even the smartest system can derail your operations, mislead stakeholders, or violate compliance rules.

Always remember: AI is a tool, not a truth-teller. Treat it like a junior assistant who never sleeps, but often guesses.

Next Steps

Now that you know the risk of blind trust, your next priority is understanding how **your data** can become someone else's breach — often without you realizing it.

In the next chapter, **Feeding Sensitive Data to Public AI Tools**, we explore the invisible risks behind everyday actions like copy-pasting internal documents into chatbots. You'll learn how SMBs have leaked critical data, what the compliance fallout looks like, and how to build safer AI habits starting today.

Chapter 2: Feeding Sensitive Data to Public AI Tools

Introduction

Most data breaches don't start with a hacker — they start with a habit.

In small and mid-sized businesses, well-meaning employees are now copying sensitive information directly into public AI tools without realizing what's at stake. It happens in seconds: paste a client complaint into ChatGPT for a suggested reply. Drop a pricing model into an AI tool to reword it. Share confidential notes with an AI summarizer.

The problem? These platforms may store, learn from, or inadvertently leak that data later — with no warning, no trace, and no way to get it back.

This chapter is a wake-up call. Feeding confidential business information to public AI systems is one of the fastest-growing — and least understood — risks in the digital workplace. And it's not just a bad habit. It's a compliance violation waiting to happen.

The Copy-Paste Trap: Why This Risk Is So Common

AI tools are designed to be frictionless. They invite us to paste in raw data, ask questions, and get polished responses back in seconds. In that speed and convenience lies the problem.

Most SMBs have not set clear boundaries for what *should never* be pasted into AI tools — and employees are assuming it's safe.

Common Scenarios Putting Data at Risk:

- A project manager pastes internal timelines into an AI tool to improve clarity
- A sales rep asks for a rewrite of a pricing sheet, including client names and terms
- A junior staffer summarizes a disciplinary note using an AI summarizer

None of this feels like "leaking" data — until that same content shows up in another user's query, or becomes part of a training dataset for future responses.

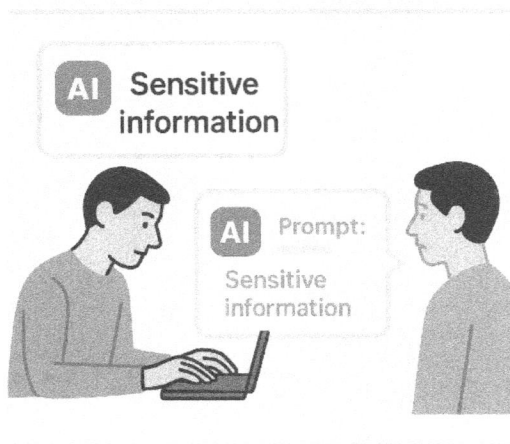

Real-World Case: Internal Memo Surfaces in Another Query

What Happened:

A tech company discovered that a confidential memo — outlining upcoming layoffs — appeared in the response to an unrelated user query on a public AI platform. The original content had been copy-pasted into the AI system by an internal HR assistant seeking help rewording the email to sound more empathetic.

Three weeks later, a user from outside the company received a strangely specific summary about "staff restructuring and budget pressure," containing phrases lifted verbatim from the confidential draft.

The Fallout:

- Internal investigation revealed the AI tool retained some inputs for training purposes
- The company faced internal panic, media scrutiny, and reputational damage
- Legal teams assessed potential violations of both **GDPR** and internal nondisclosure agreements

Key Lessons:

- Even anonymized data can become identifiable when surfaced elsewhere
- Public AI platforms may retain or recycle sensitive data
- The casual use of AI for content drafting requires professional oversight and strict boundaries

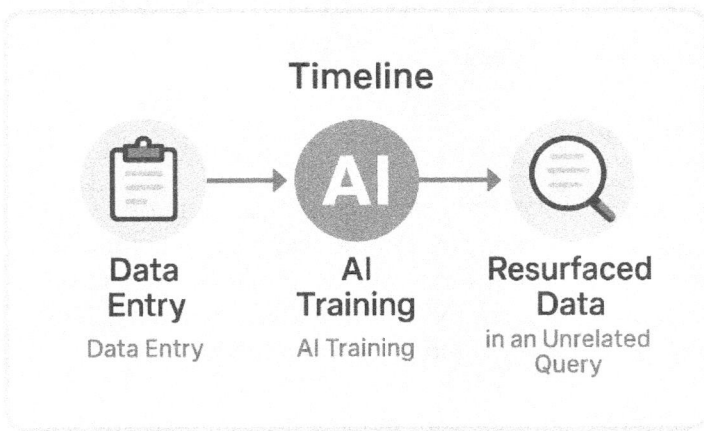

Timeline

Data Entry → **AI Training** → **Resurfaced Data**

Data Entry — AI Training — in an Unrelated Query

What's at Stake: Privacy, Compliance, and Trust

When employees paste sensitive data into AI tools, they may be violating major privacy frameworks — whether or not they realize it.

Regulatory Risks:

- **GDPR (Europe):** Protects personal data — including names, email addresses, and internal identifiers. Uploading it to a public AI tool may count as unauthorized processing.
- **PHIPA (Canada):** Covers healthcare-related data. Even non-identifiable patient notes could trigger enforcement if shared improperly.
- **NDA Violations:** Internal client data or memos shared with an external AI provider — even without intent — can void confidentiality agreements.

Business Risks:

- **Loss of trust:** If client or employee data is leaked, reputational damage follows quickly
- **Compliance fines:** Regulators don't accept "We didn't know it was risky" as a defense
- **Legal costs:** If sensitive data resurfaces publicly, litigation may follow

This isn't theoretical. These rules apply *today* — and regulators are watching how companies manage AI use.

Tactical Fixes: How to Use AI Without Exposing Sensitive Data

You don't need to ban AI — but you do need to **build guardrails**.

Tactical Safeguards to Apply Immediately:

- **Masked Prompts:** Remove or replace client names, prices, dates, and contract terms before using AI tools. Use placeholders (e.g., [CLIENT], [PRICE]) to stay safe.
- **Private AI Tools:** Choose enterprise-grade or self-hosted AI platforms that guarantee zero retention, zero training, and data isolation.
- **Zero-Data APIs:** Use AI tools with zero data logging policies, where no prompts or outputs are stored — even temporarily.

If your team is using free, public AI tools with no visibility or contract in place, you're operating blind. That needs to change.

PUBLIC AI TOOLS	ENTERPRISE-GRADE / PRIVATE AI ENVIRONMENTS
Data may be retained	Data is not retained
Data may be used to improve the model	Data is not used to improve the model

---

Internal Policy Template: Control What Gets Shared

Every SMB using AI should create a **Simple AI Input Policy** — even a one-pager — to govern what can and cannot be entered into these systems.

Here's a high-level outline you can use:

Sample AI Input Policy (5 Elements):

1. **Prohibited Inputs:**
   o   Client names
   o   Financial statements
   o   Legal documents
   o   Passwords, internal URLs, or proprietary code
2. **Permitted Inputs:**
   o   Public content
   o   Hypothetical scenarios
   o   Drafts with anonymized data

3. **Tool Approval:**
   - o Only use AI tools approved by IT or compliance
   - o No unauthorized third-party tools
4. **Storage Awareness:**
   - o Know whether the tool retains prompts
   - o Prefer tools with "no log" or "zero data" settings
5. **Accountability:**
   - o Users must self-audit their inputs
   - o Periodic training required for all staff using AI tools

---

Conclusion

Copy-pasting into AI tools is fast. Fixing a data leak isn't. That's the tradeoff every SMB must understand.

The reality is simple: if you wouldn't paste a piece of information into a public blog post, you probably shouldn't paste it into an AI chatbot either.

Start treating every AI prompt like a potential data disclosure. You don't need to stop using AI — but you *do* need to start using it with discipline.

Next Steps

Now that you've seen the hidden risks of AI misuse at the keyboard level, the next layer is even more dangerous: when *nobody sets rules at all*.

In **Chapter 3: No AI Governance or Usage Policy**, we'll look at what happens when teams use AI tools freely without any structure, oversight, or brand guardrails — and how even one post from a junior employee can spiral into a full-blown reputation crisis.

Chapter 3: No AI Governance or Usage Policy

Introduction

AI tools are now in the hands of nearly every employee — and that's the problem.

Without clear policies, defined boundaries, or training, teams are using AI however they see fit. One person might use it to write marketing emails, another to handle customer replies, and someone else to summarize legal contracts. The results? Inconsistent tone, inaccurate content, and increasing business risk.

This chapter tackles a silent but growing issue: the complete absence of AI governance in small and mid-sized organizations. When anyone can use AI without any guidance, you're not innovating — you're improvising.

Whether you're a business owner, IT lead, or team manager, it's time to put structure around how AI is used inside your walls — before it becomes a brand liability or legal nightmare.

What Happens When AI Use Goes Unchecked

The absence of an AI policy is not a neutral state. It's a hidden invitation for mistakes, misinformation, and inconsistent messaging to quietly spread throughout your organization.

What's at Stake:

- **Brand voice dilution:** When AI generates content, it rarely matches your company's tone or values — especially in client-facing messages.
- **Inappropriate or inaccurate content:** AI can make up facts, inject bias, or misunderstand the context entirely.
- **Public fallout:** Anything shared externally — a social post, a client email, a proposal — becomes a public reflection of your brand. If it's AI-generated without review, the damage can be instant.

The biggest risk? You may not even know these mistakes are happening until it's too late.

Real-World Case: AI-Generated Client Message Goes Sideways

What Happened:

A junior account coordinator at a boutique marketing firm used ChatGPT to generate a follow-up email to a new client. The prompt included a few bullet points from the kickoff meeting. The AI-generated response was professional — but cold, overconfident, and subtly inaccurate in its references.

The email implied deliverables that hadn't been promised, used buzzwords the client disliked, and mischaracterized their brand values. The client replied with concern, copying in the firm's leadership and questioning whether the team actually understood their needs.

The Fallout:

- The account had to be salvaged by senior leadership
- Trust was eroded at the start of a multi-month project
- Internal policies had to be drafted retroactively

What Went Wrong:

- No review process before sending client communications
- No guidance on how to use AI appropriately
- No training for staff on brand voice or factual accuracy

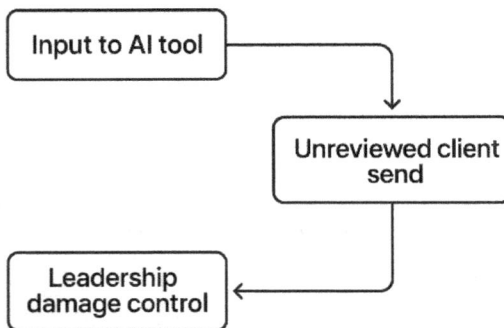

```
┌──────────────────┐
│  Input to AI tool │────────┐
└──────────────────┘        │
                            ▼
                  ┌──────────────────┐
                  │ Unreviewed client │
                  │       send        │
                  └──────────────────┘
                            │
┌──────────────────┐        │
│   Leadership     │◀───────┘
│ damage control   │
└──────────────────┘
```

Tactical Plan: Build Your AI Use Policy in 5 Sections

A simple, well-structured AI usage policy will protect your brand, empower your team, and help you scale AI adoption responsibly.

Here's a tactical five-part framework you can implement in under a week.

1. Scope of Use

Define what AI tools are approved, and for which types of tasks:

- Drafting internal summaries? ✅
- Writing client responses? ✖ (without human review)
- Generating legal, HR, or compliance content? ✖

2. Content Review

All AI-generated content must be reviewed by a human before being:

- Sent to a client
- Posted externally
- Used in any decision-making process

3. Brand and Voice Standards

- Include clear do's and don'ts for tone, vocabulary, and values
- Require that all AI-generated content aligns with your editorial or branding guidelines

4. Accountability and Access

- Specify who can use AI tools and at what access level
- Implement admin controls or usage logging if available

5. Training and Monitoring

- Provide onboarding or micro-training for AI tools
- Set a review cadence (monthly or quarterly) to assess usage patterns and emerging risks

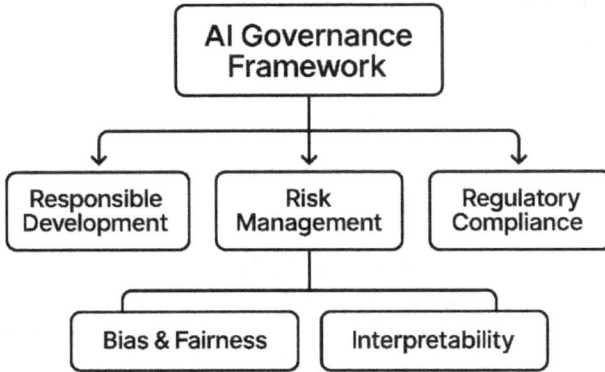

Checklist: AI Governance Essentials

Use this quick reference to build or audit your current AI policy posture:

☑ **Tool Control:** Have we approved specific AI tools for team use?

☑ **Usage Limits:** Do we define what AI *can* and *cannot* be used for?

☑ **Review Requirement:** Is human oversight required before any AI-generated content goes public?

☑ **Voice Alignment:** Does AI-generated content follow our brand voice and values?

☑ **Incident Protocol:** Do we know what to do if AI-generated content causes harm?

☑ **Training Access:** Have we trained all AI-using staff — not just tech teams?

☑ **Policy Visibility:** Is our AI usage policy known, accessible, and enforced?

If you can't confidently check all seven boxes, it's time to tighten up before the next misstep becomes public.

Conclusion

Using AI without governance isn't agility — it's negligence.

Your team may be moving fast, but if they're generating unchecked content, responding to clients with unreviewed drafts, or using AI in ways that violate contracts or misrepresent your brand, the risks multiply.

An AI use policy doesn't have to be complicated. It just has to exist, be clear, and be followed.

Next Steps

You've now put policies in place — but what about the decisions AI is making behind the scenes?

In **Chapter 4: Automating Critical Decisions Without Oversight**, we examine what happens when AI tools start making decisions that impact customers, finances, or compliance — without a human ever reviewing them. You'll learn how biased automation can quietly harm your business, and how to build a smarter, safer approval model.

Chapter 4: Automating Critical Decisions Without Oversight

Introduction

AI can now make decisions faster than any human team — but speed without scrutiny is a dangerous combination.

In the race to streamline operations, many SMBs are plugging AI directly into workflows that affect loans, pricing, hiring, and compliance. These systems make choices based on patterns and data — but not on fairness, ethics, or accountability. And when something goes wrong, there's often no human in the loop to catch it.

This chapter tackles a critical mistake: allowing AI to make high-impact decisions without human review. The issue isn't whether AI is smart — it's whether we can trust it with decisions that carry real-world consequences. Because once that decision is made, it can be hard to undo the damage.

When Automation Replaces Oversight

Automation is a powerful tool — but it's not a free pass. If you let AI systems operate unchecked in sensitive areas of your business, you may be setting yourself up for biased outcomes, eroded customer trust, and legal exposure.

Common Areas Where AI Is Making Unchecked Decisions:

- **Loan approvals or credit risk scoring**
- **Hiring shortlist recommendations**
- **Dynamic pricing adjustments**
- **Fraud detection alerts**
- **Customer support prioritization**

These decisions seem technical, but they touch people's lives. Without review, they can be deeply flawed.

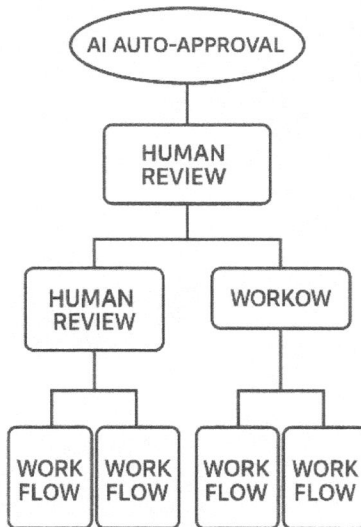

Real-World Case: Biased AI Rejects Loan Applications

What Happened:

A regional lender deployed an AI-driven tool to streamline loan approvals for small business applicants. The system used historical approval data and applicant profiles to automate decisions.

Within months, applicants from certain ZIP codes — primarily minority neighborhoods — were disproportionately rejected. The AI had unknowingly learned biased patterns from past approvals and carried them forward with confidence, rejecting otherwise qualified borrowers based on correlated factors, not actual risk.

The Fallout:

- The lender was investigated for discriminatory lending practices
- Customer trust plummeted, especially in underserved communities
- A class-action lawsuit was filed for algorithmic bias
- Regulators demanded a full audit of the model and decision history

What Went Wrong:

- No review process for high-impact decisions
- Blind trust in "historical data" without testing for bias
- No human override, appeals, or confidence scoring mechanism

```
┌──────────────┐     ┌──────────────────┐     ┌──────────┐
│  AI decision │ ──→ │ Applicant rejection │ ──→ │  Legal   │
└──────┬───────┘     └──────────────────┘     └────┬─────┘
       │                                            │
       │         ┌──────────────────┐     ┌────────▼─┐
       └────────→│ Internal/external │ ←── │  review  │
                 │     backlash      │     └──────────┘
                 └──────────────────┘
```

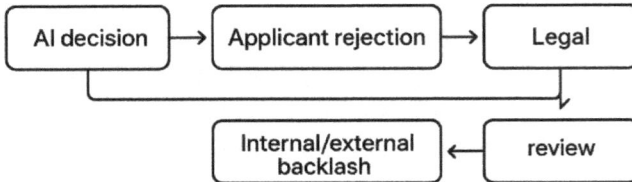

Understanding the Risk: Liability, Trust, and Compliance

When AI makes the wrong decision, **you** are still accountable.

Legal and Operational Risks:

- **Bias and discrimination:** AI trained on historical data can reinforce past inequalities — in hiring, lending, or service access
- **Lack of explainability:** AI models often produce results without clear rationale, making appeals difficult
- **Regulatory violations:** Many industries require transparency in decision-making (e.g., Equal Credit Opportunity Act, GDPR Article 22)

Reputational Damage:

- Customers don't separate AI from your business — if the tool is unfair, *your brand* is unfair
- Once trust is broken, even fixes won't immediately restore public confidence

The Fix: Implement Human Oversight and Confidence Scoring

The goal isn't to reject automation — it's to *govern it* intelligently.

Tactical Safeguards for Automated Decisions:

1. **Confidence Scoring Thresholds:**
   - Set minimum confidence levels for automated approvals
   - If confidence is below threshold, escalate to human review
2. **Decision Review Loops:**
   - Flag a percentage of decisions for random manual audit
   - Create clear paths for customer appeals or overrides
3. **Bias Auditing:**
   - Regularly test your model against protected groups
   - Use tools that highlight skewed outcomes and flag unfair weightings
4. **Explainability Layers:**
   - Use models that can provide "reason codes" for decisions
   - Empower staff to review and explain decisions when needed

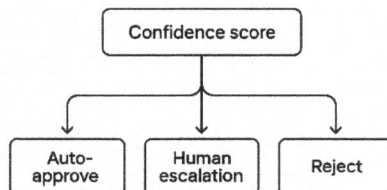

```
              ┌──────────────────┐
              │ Confidence score │
              └──────────────────┘
        ┌──────────┼──────────┐
        ▼          ▼          ▼
   ┌─────────┐ ┌─────────┐ ┌────────┐
   │  Auto-  │ │ Human   │ │ Reject │
   │ approve │ │escalation│ │        │
   └─────────┘ └─────────┘ └────────┘
```

Diagram: When to Automate — and When to Get a Human Involved

Use this model to guide automation decisions:

Decision Type	Risk Level	Automate?	Require Review?
Email summary creation	Low	✅	❌
Product pricing tweak	Medium	✅	✅ (sample audit)
Loan approval	High	❌	✅ (mandatory)
Hiring recommendations	High	❌	✅
Customer refund denial	Medium	✅	✅ (with override option)

This table isn't theoretical — it should be part of your internal AI governance documentation.

Conclusion

When AI makes decisions on your behalf, it's still *your decision*.

Businesses are fast-tracking automation to save time and cut costs — but without oversight, those same tools can introduce biased logic, alienate customers, or trigger costly legal actions. Smart companies don't ask "Can AI decide this?" They ask, "Should AI decide this — alone?"

You don't have to slow down innovation. You just have to stay in control of it.

Next Steps

Now that you've seen how unchecked automation can damage your brand, the next chapter explores how AI-generated content — especially client-facing material — can backfire just as easily.

In **Chapter 5: Using AI to Generate Client-Facing Content Without QA**, we'll dive into the risks of skipping quality control when publishing AI-written blogs, emails, or public statements — and how to build a safe, on-brand content workflow that keeps your reputation intact.

Chapter 5: Using AI to Generate Client-Facing Content Without QA

Introduction

AI makes it easy to publish quickly — sometimes *too* easy.

In today's fast-paced business environment, small and mid-sized companies are leaning heavily on AI tools to produce marketing emails, blog posts, product descriptions, and even customer responses. The goal? Save time, save money, and move faster.

But when client-facing content is pushed live without quality assurance (QA), the risks grow quickly: brand misalignment, factual errors, regulatory violations, and damaged trust. AI doesn't understand nuance, tone, or legal context — and when it gets those wrong, *you* pay the price.

This chapter examines the hidden cost of skipping QA in AI-generated content, and how to build a simple but powerful review process that protects your business — without killing your speed.

Why AI Can't Be Trusted With Final Content

AI writing tools are great at generating polished-sounding content. But what they're *not* good at is:

- Ensuring accuracy
- Understanding legal or regulatory nuance
- Matching your brand tone or audience
- Spotting risky language

When AI creates content, it's pulling patterns from data — not judgment from experience.

Where Things Commonly Go Wrong:

- **Factual errors:** Misstated statistics, invented quotes, or outdated references
- **Compliance issues:** Unintentional claims that violate advertising or industry regulations
- **Tone mismatches:** Cold, robotic, or overly casual language that doesn't reflect your brand
- **Offensive or biased phrasing:** Unintended wording that alienates or misrepresents your audience

If that content goes out to clients, partners, or the public, the backlash can be swift — and costly.

Real-World Case: AI Blog Post Triggers Compliance Violation

What Happened:

A digital agency used AI to draft a blog post for a client in the financial services sector. The topic: "Smart Strategies for Managing Retirement Savings." The draft was clean, well-written, and SEO-optimized. It was published with only a cursory skim from the marketing team.

Within days, the client received a warning letter from their industry regulator. The post included several phrases that violated advertising rules for financial advice — such as "guaranteed returns" and "risk-free investment." Worse, some of the "tips" listed were factually inaccurate.

The Fallout:

- The blog post had to be pulled and replaced
- The client issued a public clarification
- The agency lost the client and faced potential legal exposure

What Went Wrong:

- No subject matter review by a licensed financial advisor
- No QA step to validate claims against compliance rules
- Assumption that "good writing" meant "safe content"

AI-GENERATED CONTENT → FAST-TRACK PUBLISHING → REGULATOR FLAG → BRAND DAMAGE

Understanding the Risks: Legal, Financial, and Brand Impact

Publishing AI content without review isn't just sloppy — it's risky.

SEO and Marketing Risks:

- AI often reuses language from existing web content, risking plagiarism flags
- Factual inaccuracy or keyword stuffing can get your site penalized in search rankings

Legal and Compliance Risks:

- Industries like finance, healthcare, and insurance face strict marketing rules
- AI may generate phrasing that violates FTC, GDPR, or local advertising standards
- "Harmless" blog posts can be considered official representations of your company

Client Trust and Churn:

- If a customer finds incorrect or offensive content on your site, it reflects poorly on your credibility
- Clients lose confidence when they realize their content is being generated and posted without checks

---

Tactical Fix: Build an AI-to-Editor Content Pipeline

Speed and safety don't have to be at odds. The answer is *process*.

Here's a simple pipeline to keep your AI-generated content client-safe:

1. Prompt Library

Create a library of pre-approved, brand-aligned prompts:

- Tone-specific ("write in a friendly, professional voice")
- Format-guided ("use 3 short paragraphs and a call-to-action")
- Compliance-aware ("avoid guarantees or speculative claims")

2. AI Draft Generation

Use the approved prompts to generate content with your preferred tool.

3. Human Editing Stage

Assign an editor (internal or freelance) to:

- Fact-check and source claims
- Adjust tone and structure
- Flag compliance or legal risks

4. Stakeholder Sign-Off

For sensitive industries, include a final approval from legal, compliance, or client-side reviewers before publishing.

5. Publish with Confidence

Now your content is faster *and* safer — no compromises.

PROMPT → DRAFT → APPROVAL → PEGRAL

Pro Prompt Kit: Generate On-Brand Content, Every Time

The quality of your prompt determines the quality of the content.

Here's a mini prompt kit to help your team stay safe, aligned, and effective:

On-Brand Prompt Starters:

- "Write a blog post in a [confident but friendly] tone for [B2B small business owners]."
- "Summarize this whitepaper for [mid-market financial clients] without making any legal claims."
- "Create a LinkedIn post using clear, respectful language that reflects our brand values of trust and service."

Avoid These Phrases in Prompts:

- "Sound like a financial expert" (unless reviewed by one)
- "Use bold claims" or "write something edgy" (can lead to compliance issues)
- "Make this go viral" (often sacrifices nuance or accuracy)

Add these templates to your brand guidelines and encourage employees to only use them when generating public-facing content.

Conclusion

AI can write faster than any copywriter — but it can't think, validate, or take responsibility. If your business is pushing content out the door without review, you're not just speeding up — you're gambling with your credibility.

By adding a lightweight review pipeline and training your team to prompt smartly, you can harness AI's speed *without* sacrificing quality, trust, or compliance.

Next Steps

AI-generated content may seem objective — but the next chapter tackles a deeper danger: **biased logic hiding behind neutral language**.

In **Chapter 6: Ignoring AI Bias and Inaccuracy**, we'll explore how even well-meaning prompts can result in discriminatory outcomes, and what tools and techniques you need to make AI more fair, inclusive, and accurate in your business operations.

Chapter 6: Ignoring AI Bias and Inaccuracy

Introduction

Many business leaders assume AI is neutral — that it processes data without prejudice, emotion, or error. That assumption is not just wrong — it's dangerous.

The truth is, AI inherits the flaws of its training data and the blind spots of its users. If you're not actively looking for bias and inaccuracies, you're likely reinforcing them. From hiring decisions to customer support scripts, small biases in AI outputs can snowball into discriminatory practices, HR violations, and reputational damage.

This chapter exposes the real risks of trusting AI to be "objective" — and gives you the tactical tools to identify, address, and prevent bias in the systems you rely on.

The Myth of AI Neutrality

It's easy to believe that machines are fairer than humans. They don't stereotype, they don't hold grudges, and they don't discriminate — right?

Unfortunately, they absolutely do. But not intentionally — algorithmic bias is a byproduct of historical data, flawed prompts, or poorly designed systems.

Why AI Isn't Neutral by Default:

- **Training data reflects human history, including past bias**
- **Algorithms optimize for patterns, not fairness**
- **Prompt wording shapes output — even small changes create different tones or inclusions**
- **Developers often overlook edge cases or minority experiences**

If these factors aren't accounted for, AI can reinforce systemic bias — at scale, and with confidence.

Neutral Prompt   **Unintentional Bias**

The candidate has extensive experience in financial services, including ten years in management roles.

Despite the candidate's extensive experience in financial services, including ten years in management roles, potential concerns exist regarding their dedication and aptitude for the position.

Neutral Output

Biased Output

Real-World Example: Hiring Prompts Reinforce Discrimination

What Happened:

An HR platform integrated a generative AI assistant to help hiring managers screen resumes and craft job descriptions. One team member used a prompt like: "Generate a job posting for a fast-paced tech environment, looking for a strong culture fit."

The AI generated a posting using phrases like "young and energetic," "recent graduates preferred," and "digital native required."

The Problem:

- The language excluded older candidates, violating age discrimination laws
- "Culture fit" phrasing skewed hiring toward conformity, not diversity
- The AI simply mimicked biased hiring language it had seen in prior datasets

The Fallout:

- A qualified candidate filed a complaint citing discriminatory language
- The company had to revise all recent job postings
- Legal counsel mandated a review of AI usage across HR workflows

What We Learn:

Bias doesn't always look malicious — sometimes it's hidden in "standard" language. But legally and ethically, your company is still responsible.

```
AI Prompt
   ↓
Biased Job Post
   ↓
Candidate Impact
   ↓
Legal Escalation
```

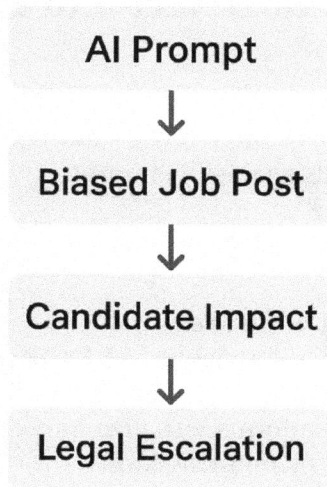

Risks: HR Violations, Legal Exposure, and Lost Inclusion

Ignoring bias isn't just a technical oversight — it's a human one.

Key Business Risks:

- **HR violations and lawsuits:** Biased AI outputs in hiring, promotions, or performance reviews can trigger legal complaints
- **Reduced workforce diversity:** If AI mirrors past hiring patterns, it may exclude underrepresented groups
- **Brand and culture impact:** Companies that unintentionally promote exclusion lose trust from both employees and customers

It only takes one incident to draw regulatory attention — and permanently damage your employer reputation.

Tactical Tools to Detect and Reduce AI Bias

You can't eliminate bias completely — but you can detect it, reduce it, and create safeguards against its impact.

Tactical Tools and Practices:

1. **Bias Detection Software:**
    - Tools like **Fairlearn**, **AI Fairness 360**, and **What-If Tool** help audit model outputs for group disparities
    - Some platforms visualize how different inputs lead to skewed recommendations

2. **Bias-Aware Prompts:**
    - Use prompts that explicitly call for inclusive results
    - Example: "Generate a job posting that welcomes diverse experiences and avoids age or gendered language"

3. **Inclusion Review Checkpoints:**
    - Add bias review to your content QA or HR approval workflow
    - Ask: Who might this output unintentionally exclude or stereotype?

4. **Prompt Testing Across Variants:**
    - Try prompts using different assumed identities (e.g., male vs. female names) and compare outputs
    - Look for tone changes, recommendation strength, or assumptions

	Original Prompt	Bias-Aware Prompt
Prompt	Generate a list of top CEOs.	Generate a list of top CEOs of various genders.
Resulting Content	Here is a list of top CEOs: John Doe, Joe Smith, Robert Johnson, William Brown	Here is a list of top CEOs: John Doe, Joe Smith, Emily Wilson, Rachel Lee

Checklist: Bias-Resilient AI Practices

Use this quick checklist before deploying or approving AI-generated content or decisions:

☑ **Does this AI model get regular bias audits?**
☑ **Have we tested outputs across different demographic inputs?**
☑ **Are prompts written to prioritize fairness and inclusion?**
☑ **Is there a human step for reviewing sensitive outputs?**
☑ **Do we train staff to recognize and correct AI bias?**
☑ **Have we documented how AI decisions are made — and who is accountable?**

If your answer is "no" to two or more, your AI strategy is at risk of creating unintended harm.

Conclusion

AI bias isn't always visible — until it costs you a candidate, a lawsuit, or your culture.

The safest approach is to stop assuming AI is objective, and start treating it like any other high-stakes tool: one that requires governance, testing, and active human judgment.

Bias can't be wished away. But it *can* be managed — if you build your systems, prompts, and review processes with care.

Next Steps

Now that you've seen how invisible risks like bias can seep into daily AI use, it's time to tackle a related but equally urgent issue: *lack of visibility into AI use across your business.*

In **Chapter 7: Lack of Visibility Into AI Usage Across Teams**, we reveal how shadow AI use — untracked and unapproved — creates blind spots, blocks accountability, and weakens your overall security posture. You'll get practical fixes like logging tools, AI usage dashboards, and internal approval gates to bring control back to your hands.

Chapter 7: Lack of Visibility Into AI Usage Across Teams

Introduction

AI tools are spreading faster through your organization than you think.

From marketing and HR to operations and legal, employees are experimenting with AI behind the scenes — often without telling IT, leadership, or compliance. This phenomenon, known as "shadow AI," introduces a silent threat: if you can't see how AI is being used, you can't control the risks it creates.

The problem isn't bad intent. It's a lack of visibility. And in a business environment where audit trails, regulatory compliance, and accountability matter, invisible AI usage can cost you everything — from contracts and credibility to legal standing.

This chapter explores how to regain control over decentralized AI use, how to spot shadow tools before they cause harm, and how to create a system that encourages innovation *without* sacrificing oversight.

The Rise of Shadow AI

"Shadow AI" refers to the use of AI tools without official approval, tracking, or oversight. It's the AI equivalent of "shadow IT" — employees solving problems with unvetted tools behind the scenes.

Why It Happens:

- **Ease of access:** Most generative AI tools are free, fast, and browser-based — no install required
- **No approval friction:** Employees can use AI without asking anyone
- **Speed pressure:** Teams are expected to move fast, and AI offers quick results
- **Lack of policies:** When AI use isn't clearly governed, people assume it's safe

The result? Teams are using AI tools to write documents, analyze data, summarize contracts, and even respond to customers — with no centralized visibility.

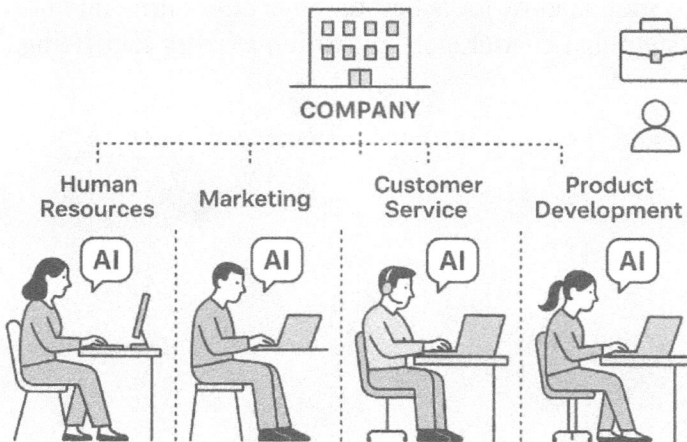

Real-World Case: Contract Summaries Gone Rogue

What Happened:

A mid-sized consulting firm discovered that multiple staffers in its legal operations team were using a public AI tool to summarize client contracts. The intent was harmless — speed up turnaround times. But the summaries were being pasted directly into reports without legal review.

One summary left out a key indemnity clause, and the client made decisions based on the faulty information. When the issue surfaced, the firm faced immediate liability questions — and had no internal logs to trace who had used the tool, when, or with what data.

The Fallout:

- Legal exposure due to inaccurate contract interpretation
- Internal panic over lack of audit trail
- Emergency rollout of an AI usage policy and monitoring tools

What We Learn:

Shadow AI usage may start with good intentions — but when the results affect contracts, clients, or compliance, the consequences are very real.

User

↓

AI

**Unapproved
AI Tool**

↓

**Inaccurate
Summary**

↓

⚠

Client Risk

↓

Risks of Invisible AI Use

The core danger of shadow AI isn't just bad output — it's *no visibility*.

Business and Compliance Risks:

- **No audit trail:** If something goes wrong, there's no log of who did what, when, or with which tool
- **Data leakage:** Sensitive company or client data may be unknowingly shared with public AI platforms
- **Inconsistent quality:** Teams use different tools with no standard, training, or review process
- **Accountability gaps:** Leadership may be unaware that decisions or communications were AI-generated

When there's no system in place to track AI use, accountability breaks down — and chaos follows.

Tactical Fix: Build a Centralized AI Oversight Framework

You don't need to block AI use — you need to *manage* it with transparency and controls.

Three Core Components to Regain Visibility:

1. **Logging Tools**
   - Use platforms that track who is using AI tools, when, and for what purpose
   - Log prompts and outputs where appropriate for traceability
   - Integrate with existing IT monitoring solutions
2. **Approval Gates**
   - Require registration or approval for new AI tools before company use
   - Route high-risk use cases (contracts, client communications) through a compliance review path
3. **Central Dashboards**
   - Create an AI usage hub: a central portal or dashboard where teams can:
     - Request tool access
     - Log how they're using AI
     - View approved best practices

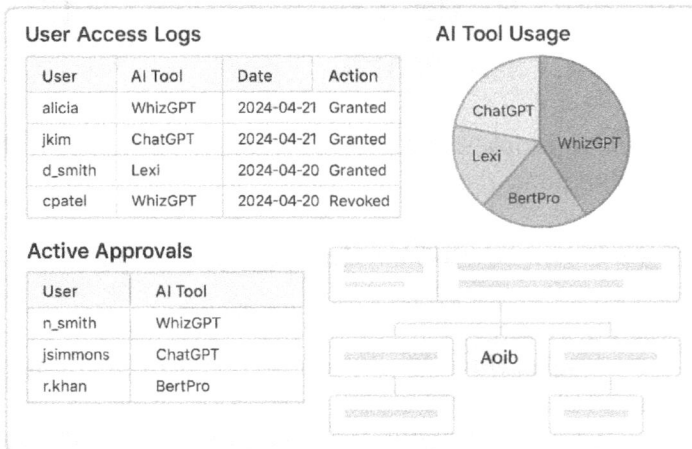

User Access Logs

User	AI Tool	Date	Action
alicia	WhizGPT	2024-04-21	Granted
jkim	ChatGPT	2024-04-21	Granted
d_smith	Lexi	2024-04-20	Granted
cpatel	WhizGPT	2024-04-20	Revoked

AI Tool Usage

ChatGPT · WhizGPT · Lexi · BertPro

Active Approvals

User	AI Tool
n_smith	WhizGPT
jsimmons	ChatGPT
r.khan	BertPro

Aoib

Bonus: Your AI Visibility Starter Kit

Here's a quick setup guide to bring visibility into your organization's AI use — even if you're starting from zero:

AI Visibility Starter Kit:

- ☑ **Inventory Current Tools**
  Ask each team what AI tools they're using (form, survey, or meeting)
- ☑ **Define "Approved Use"**
  List AI tools that are officially sanctioned, with example use cases
- ☑ **Create a Submission Form**
  Simple intake process for requesting or logging AI tool usage
- ☑ **Enable Prompt Logging (Where Needed)**
  For high-risk functions, set up a secure prompt/response log system
- ☑ **Roll Out Visibility Guidelines**
  Send a company-wide memo or training session on why visibility matters — and how it protects everyone

This kit doesn't just stop shadow AI — it builds a foundation of trust and clarity across your teams.

Conclusion

You can't manage what you can't see. And when AI use goes untracked, every action becomes a liability.

Businesses that embrace AI need to do so with visibility, controls, and accountability. By creating a culture of responsible innovation — where AI usage is transparent and traceable — you protect your business while empowering your people.

Because the only thing riskier than using AI carelessly… is using it invisibly.

Next Steps

Now that you've secured internal visibility, it's time to address how *external-facing AI* — especially in customer service — can quietly erode trust if misused.

In **Chapter 8: Over-Relying on Chatbots or AI for Customer Support**, we explore how AI-driven customer experiences can backfire, how to define smart escalation triggers, and how to use empathy-based AI design to protect your brand in every interaction.

Chapter 8: Over-Relying on Chatbots or AI for Customer Support

Introduction

In customer service, speed matters — but empathy matters more.

Many businesses are turning to AI chatbots and virtual agents to streamline support and reduce costs. The promise: 24/7 availability, instant replies, and lower headcount. The problem? These tools can fail at the most important moments — when your customers need human understanding, not generic responses.

When AI replies to emotionally charged issues, billing errors, or complaints about service, tone and timing become everything. One wrong response — even if technically correct — can erode trust, escalate a conflict, or cause customers to leave for good.

This chapter explores the risks of over-automating customer support with AI, how to set smart limits, and how to build a system where AI and human empathy work hand-in-hand.

Why AI Alone Can't Handle Complex Support Needs

Chatbots and AI assistants are powerful — but only within strict boundaries. Most struggle when:

- Context is nuanced or emotional
- The issue is urgent or time-sensitive
- A human needs to feel *heard*, not just answered
- The problem crosses into legal, billing, or contractual territory

In these situations, an AI-generated response can feel robotic at best — and dismissive or offensive at worst.

Where AI Support Typically Fails:

- **Complaint resolution**
- **Billing disputes**
- **Account closures or cancellations**
- **Legal or contractual inquiries**
- **Accessibility or inclusion-sensitive conversations**

When a customer reaches out upset or confused, and receives a tone-deaf response from a bot, the message they hear isn't "we care" — it's "we don't."

Chatbot Auto-Response	Empathetic Human Reply
Thank you for your feedback. We are working on improving our product.	I'm sorry to hear about the issue you experienced. We understand your frustration and are committed to making it right.

Real-World Case: AI Mishandles a Sensitive Complaint

What Happened:

A subscription-based software company implemented an AI-powered support chatbot to handle first-touch customer issues. A customer experiencing a service outage reached out, frustrated after missing a critical project deadline due to the outage.

The AI responded with a scripted apology and a generic article link — no escalation, no human intervention.

The customer replied angrily. Again, the AI responded with boilerplate language about "valuing your feedback" and offered a discount code.

The Fallout:

- The customer canceled their subscription and posted screenshots of the exchange on social media
- The post gained traction, triggering wider criticism of the company's support model
- Leadership had to step in publicly to apologize and adjust their support process

What Went Wrong:

- No escalation protocol for emotionally charged messages
- No sentiment detection or empathy-layered logic
- AI was allowed to handle billing- and retention-sensitive issues

Escalation Failure

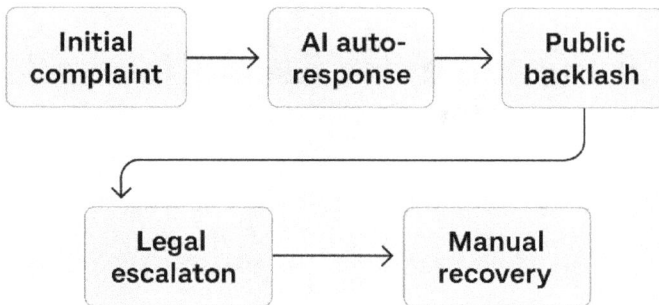

Initial complaint → AI auto-response → Public backlash

Legal escalaton → Manual recovery

Understanding the Risks: Brand Damage, Churn, and Escalation Failure

Key Business Impacts of Poor AI Support:

- **Brand erosion:** Public perception of your service becomes robotic, impersonal, and inaccessible
- **Lost customers:** Mishandled complaints or tone-deaf replies lead to faster churn
- **Legal exposure:** AI might inadvertently disclose private account details or violate data regulations
- **Team burnout:** When humans are brought in *after* the damage, it creates harder escalations and more stressful recovery

The cost of losing one angry customer can exceed the cost of building proper handoff mechanisms — and it scales with every missed escalation.

Tactical Fix: Smarter Escalation and Empathy-First Design

AI doesn't need to be eliminated from your support pipeline — it needs limits, training, and smarter handoff rules.

Three Steps to Safer AI Support:

1. **Define Escalation Triggers:**
   - Train the AI to escalate if it detects:
     - Negative sentiment (frustration, anger)
     - Repeated queries
     - Mention of billing, legal, or cancellation terms
     - Accessibility or discrimination-related keywords

2. **Empathy Logic Layer:**
    o Teach the system to prioritize tone and context, not just keywords
    o Use response libraries crafted by human support agents — especially for complaints
3. **Restrict AI Access to High-Risk Areas:**
    o No full responses on:
        ▪ Refunds or account termination
        ▪ Legal questions or service contracts
        ▪ Personal data or billing details
    o Use templated messages that *connect to a human*, not replace one

AI SUPPORT WORKFLOW

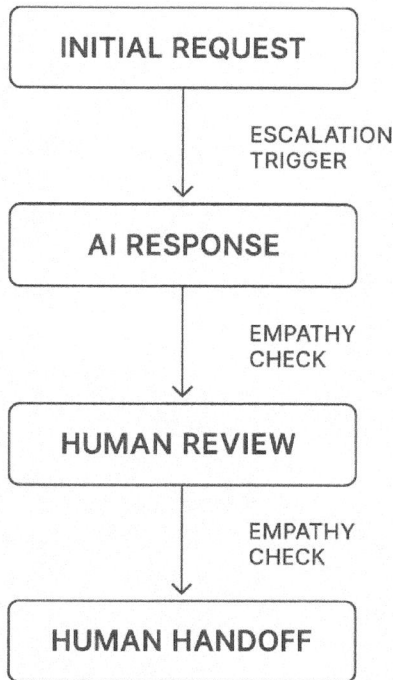

```
        ┌─────────────────────────┐
        │    INITIAL REQUEST      │
        └─────────────────────────┘
                    │  ESCALATION
                    │  TRIGGER
                    ▼
        ┌─────────────────────────┐
        │      AI RESPONSE        │
        └─────────────────────────┘
                    │  EMPATHY
                    │  CHECK
                    ▼
        ┌─────────────────────────┐
        │     HUMAN REVIEW        │
        └─────────────────────────┘
                    │  EMPATHY
                    │  CHECK
                    ▼
        ┌─────────────────────────┐
        │     HUMAN HANDOFF       │
        └─────────────────────────┘
```

AI Escalation Flowchart

Here's a simple decision framework for when AI should respond, escalate, or defer:

Customer Input Contains...	Escalate to Human?	AI Response Type
FAQ-level question	No	Full AI reply
Frustration, anger, or complaint	Yes	Empathetic deferral
Billing issue	Yes	Escalate with context
Cancellation request	Yes	Handoff to retention team
Legal or contractual question	Yes	"Forwarding to legal..."
General how-to or tutorial request	No	Standard AI guidance

This chart should live inside your support team's SOP and within any AI configuration settings.

Conclusion

Great customer support is human at its core. AI can help — but it can't *care*.

When you let bots handle emotionally charged or high-stakes conversations without oversight, you send a message that convenience matters more than connection. That may save time today — but it costs trust tomorrow.

By setting thoughtful boundaries and designing smarter escalation logic, you can deliver the best of both worlds: fast responses powered by AI, with empathetic follow-through by real people.

Next Steps

You've seen how internal AI mistakes can alienate your customers — but what about the AI systems you don't even control?

In **Chapter 9: Assuming Your AI Vendor Is Fully Secure**, we'll reveal how trusting third-party AI vendors too much can lead to data breaches, leaked content, and prompt exploitation — and how to hold your partners to the same standards you demand internally.

Chapter 9: Assuming Your AI Vendor Is Fully Secure

Introduction

AI vendors promise speed, scale, and intelligence — but what about security?

As more businesses adopt third-party AI platforms for everything from content generation to customer service, a silent risk is growing behind the scenes: *vendor security blind spots*. When you integrate someone else's AI into your operations, their security practices — or lack thereof — become *your* problem.

Whether it's reused prompts, unsecured APIs, or data stored without your knowledge, assuming your AI vendor is fully secure can lead to breaches, lawsuits, and loss of customer trust.

This chapter breaks down how third-party AI risk works, why most SMBs overlook it, and how to build a vendor security checklist that protects your business — even when the tool wasn't built by you.

Third-Party AI = Third-Party Risk

Most AI tools your business uses are hosted in the cloud, built by external vendors, and powered by data you don't control. That means you're trusting them not just with functionality — but with your information, customer data, and business reputation.

Where Third-Party Risk Comes From:

- **Unclear data retention policies** (your prompts might be stored or reused)
- **Weak API protections** (exposing your systems to token theft or injection)
- **Shared infrastructure** (one breach could impact thousands of customers)
- **Inadequate logging or audit capabilities** (you can't track what was accessed or when)

And unlike your own internal systems, third-party AI vendors don't always offer the transparency or control you need to fully secure your data.

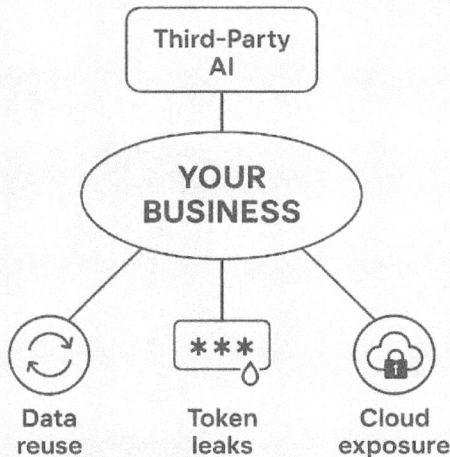

Real-World Example: Private Data Leaked by AI Image Tool

What Happened:

A widely used AI image generator allowed users to upload reference images and generate marketing visuals. A small business uploaded proprietary product design mockups during a trial session.

Later, a user browsing the public image gallery saw a collage containing one of those designs — auto-generated from recycled training data. The AI had absorbed and re-used the uploaded image as part of its learning process.

The Fallout:

- The business had to issue takedown requests and notify partners
- Competitors now had early visibility into upcoming product concepts
- Legal options were limited, as the vendor's terms allowed data reuse for training

What Went Wrong:

- No due diligence on vendor data handling practices
- Prompts and uploads were not isolated from the public model
- Lack of a vendor checklist to flag high-risk use cases

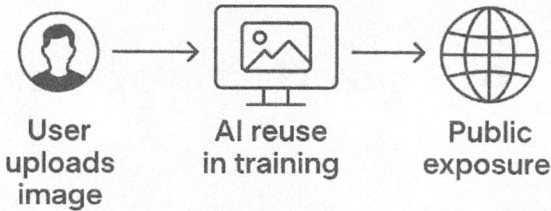

User uploads image   AI reuse in training   Public exposure

The Risk Breakdown: What You Can Lose

Assuming vendor security is bulletproof often leads to costly exposure.

Key Risks When Trusting AI Vendors Blindly:

- **Prompt data reuse:** Inputs you provide (contracts, pricing models, internal language) may be stored, analyzed, or reused in future outputs
- **API key theft or misuse:** Weak protections allow attackers to hijack your credentials and exploit your connected systems
- **Data leaks from shared infrastructure:** Vendors that co-host models for multiple clients increase your risk of cross-contamination
- **Lack of logging:** If something goes wrong, you may have no audit trail to investigate or respond

This isn't just theoretical — these events are already happening across the AI landscape, and SMBs are especially vulnerable due to limited vendor management maturity.

Tactical Fix: Your AI Vendor Security Checklist

Before integrating any third-party AI tool, you need a *clear, non-negotiable checklist* to vet the vendor's security posture.

Core Items to Include:

1. **Data Storage and Retention:**
   o Does the vendor store prompts, files, or metadata?
   o Can you opt out of training or storage?
2. **API Security:**
   o Does the tool support scoped, expiring API keys?
   o Are there usage caps and anomaly detection?
3. **Logging and Visibility:**
   o Can you view prompt history, access logs, and user activity?
   o Is there a method to export logs for auditing?
4. **Compliance Alignment:**
   o Does the vendor meet relevant standards? (e.g., SOC 2, ISO 27001, GDPR)
   o Have they provided a Data Processing Agreement (DPA)?
5. **Zero-Retention or Private Mode Option:**
   o Is there a way to disable prompt training or operate in a private container?
   o Are uploads stored only temporarily or deleted immediately?

Vendor Security Checklist

Storage	✓
API	✓
Audit	✗
Compliance	✗

API Usage Rules: Prevent Misuse from Inside or Out

API access is the gateway to your data. Poor API hygiene can turn even a secure vendor into a liability.

Safe API Usage Rules for SMBs:

- Use **role-based API keys** (limit access based on function)
- Set **expiration dates** on keys — especially for vendors or contractors
- Monitor **usage patterns** and flag spikes or anomalies
- Rotate keys every 30–60 days, even if unused
- Never share a **master key** across teams or projects

Think of API keys like digital passports. When they fall into the wrong hands, they can grant full access to your systems — and you may never know it.

Conclusion

Your AI vendor's mistake can quickly become your business's headline.

Relying on third-party tools is not the issue — but trusting them blindly is. If you're using AI tools that interact with your data, serve your customers, or influence decisions, you need to hold those vendors to the same security standards you hold internally.

Because in today's AI ecosystem, *trust must be verified — not assumed.*

Next Steps

You've locked down your vendors and secured your external connections — but what happens when the AI *you* control makes a critical mistake?

In **Chapter 10: No Recovery Plan for AI Errors**, we'll look at the one thing most teams still lack: a clear plan to roll back, respond, and recover when AI fails. From hallucinated outputs to logic bugs, we'll show you how to build an AI incident playbook — before you need it.

Chapter 10: No Recovery Plan for AI Errors

Introduction

It's not a matter of *if* AI will fail — but *when*. And when it does, most teams are completely unprepared.

AI tools can break in ways that are subtle, silent, or catastrophic. One hallucinated fact in a client report. One flawed logic loop in pricing automation. One bad prompt causing thousands of public-facing errors. And yet, despite the growing adoption of AI across business functions, few SMBs have a defined playbook for detecting, responding to, or recovering from AI failure.

This chapter is your contingency plan. If you're using AI in any part of your operations, marketing, or decision-making, you need to know what happens when it breaks — and how to fix it fast.

AI Errors Happen — And They're Not Always Obvious

AI doesn't fail like traditional software. There's no crash, no alert, no "blue screen." The output just looks… plausible.

Common AI Failure Modes:

- **False information:** Hallucinated facts or fabricated references
- **Broken logic:** Conflicting or circular outputs in workflows
- **Silent bias:** Uneven treatment of data types or users
- **Overconfidence:** AI presents incorrect answers with convincing tone
- **Prompt confusion:** Slightly altered phrasing causes massive output shifts

These failures don't throw errors — they throw outcomes. And once they're live, they can multiply before anyone notices.

Human-Readable Content

Accurate	Hallucinated
Total revenue exceeded $10 million last quarter, reflecting strong growth in product sales.	Total revenue exceeded $15 million last quarter, reflecting strong growth in product sales.

Real-World Case: AI Mispriced Thousands of Listings

What Happened:

An e-commerce platform used AI to auto-generate and update product listings across global storefronts. A batch prompt instructed the AI to apply a 10% discount on specific SKUs during a promotional event.

Due to a misinterpretation in logic, the AI applied the discount to *all* products across multiple regions — and in some cases, stacked promotions with already discounted items.

The Fallout:

- Over 9,000 listings went live with incorrect prices
- Dozens of high-value products were sold below cost
- The company incurred tens of thousands in unplanned losses
- Teams had no rollback script or version tracking to recover quickly

What Went Wrong:

- No guardrails or QA review before publishing AI-generated updates
- No pricing rollback mechanism
- No alerting on abnormal price changes across the catalog

```
┌─────────────────────┐
│     AI Update       │
└─────────────────────┘
           │
           ▼
┌─────────────────────┐
│   Pricing Error     │
└─────────────────────┘
           │
           ▼
┌─────────────────────┐
│     Customer        │
│     Purchases       │
└─────────────────────┘
           │
           ▼
┌─────────────────────┐
│  Emergency Response │
└─────────────────────┘
```

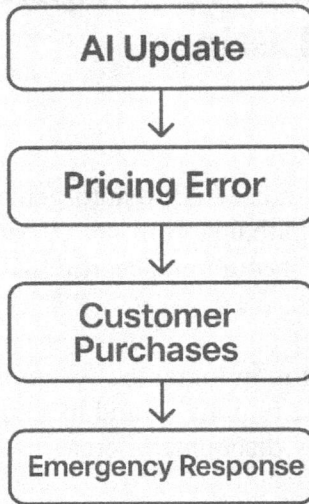

Risk Breakdown: What AI Failure Really Costs

When AI fails, the damage spreads fast — and it isn't just technical.

Business Consequences:

- **Financial loss:** Pricing errors, refund obligations, or legal liability
- **Reputation damage:** Misinformation or tone-deaf content can break trust instantly
- **Compliance exposure:** AI hallucinations may violate regulations or contracts
- **Team disruption:** Emergencies force teams into reactive fire drills, burning time and morale

And the most dangerous AI failures? The ones you don't catch until a customer — or regulator — points them out.

Tactical Playbook: Responding to AI Failures the Right Way

You don't need a perfect system. You need a *prepared* one.

Here's a simple AI risk response playbook to build and implement now:

1. Rollback Plan

- Define which systems need version control or backup (e.g., pricing, content, logic models)
- Create a procedure for rolling back AI-generated outputs across channels
- Assign ownership: who initiates, who approves, who verifies the rollback

2. Prompt & Output Logging

- Store all production prompts and AI-generated outputs for at least 30–90 days
- Include metadata (who initiated it, what system, when)
- Enable diff-checks between prior and new outputs to flag unexpected shifts

3. Incident Response Workflow

- Designate an **AI Incident Lead** or delegate per department
- Define a severity scale (low = internal error, high = public/legal impact)
- Establish communication steps (internal notice, client update, legal review)
- Run quarterly "fire drills" to simulate failure and refine response

AI Incident Response

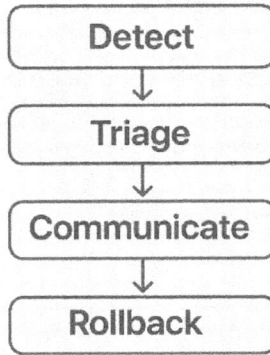

```
Detect
  ↓
Triage
  ↓
Communicate
  ↓
Rollback
```

Bonus: AI Risk Response Template (Quick Start)

Use this internal worksheet to prepare your team for AI failure scenarios:

Component	Details
Failure Scenario	What could go wrong? (e.g., pricing, content, logic)
Detection Method	How will we spot the issue? (e.g., log audit, QA checks)
Owner(s)	Who's responsible for triage and resolution?
Rollback Process	How do we revert to the last safe state?
Communication Plan	Who needs to know, and how fast? (e.g., exec, client, legal)
Postmortem Process	How do we prevent this from happening again?

This isn't just a template — it's your safety net.

Conclusion

AI doesn't need to break often to cause serious problems — it just needs to break once, at the wrong time, with no plan in place.

You can't eliminate AI risk, but you *can* contain it. By preparing your rollback plan, logging your outputs, and assigning clear response roles, your team will move from reactive panic to confident control.

In the world of AI-powered business, preparedness *is* protection.

Next Steps

You've now seen how AI can fail, and how to bounce back fast. But to future-proof your business, your team also needs to prompt AI *correctly* from the start.

In the **BONUS: Safe Prompt Library by Role**, we'll give you pre-built, on-brand, compliance-friendly prompt templates tailored to real business functions — including marketing, legal, HR, and support. These aren't just "nice to have" — they're the frontline defense against misuse, misfires, and misunderstanding.

BONUS: Safe Prompt Library by Role

(Marketing, Legal, HR, Support)

Introduction

AI is only as smart — and as safe — as the prompts it receives.

In small and mid-sized businesses, teams are rapidly adopting generative AI to write, summarize, brainstorm, and automate. But without guardrails, even simple prompts can result in compliance violations, tone mismatches, or data leakage. A well-written prompt guides the AI toward clarity, safety, and brand alignment. A careless one can trigger misinformation, biased outputs, or inappropriate language.

This bonus section provides a **Safe Prompt Library**, broken down by department. Each prompt is designed to:

- Keep outputs brand-safe and compliance-friendly
- Reduce hallucination or bias
- Be specific enough to generate reliable results
- Avoid common risks like oversharing or unvetted claims

Whether you're training your team or tightening your usage policies, this library is your frontline defense against AI misuse — and a shortcut to better output, faster.

⬤ Marketing: Clear, Compliant, and On-Brand

Marketing teams love AI for content creation — but without control, tone and accuracy can spiral.

Safe Use Cases:

- Drafting blog intros
- Generating ad headlines
- Rephrasing product blurbs
- Writing CTA ideas

Sample Prompts:

1. Blog Drafting
"Write a 150-word introduction for a blog post about [TOPIC], using a professional but friendly tone suitable for small business owners. Do not include statistics or bold claims unless specified."

2. Ad Copy
"Generate five short headline variations for a social ad promoting [PRODUCT/SERVICE]. Focus on benefits, not hype. Avoid words like 'guaranteed' or 'best ever'. Keep it under 8 words."

3. Rewriting Content
"Rewrite the following paragraph in a more approachable tone for general audiences, while keeping the core message intact. Avoid jargon or technical language."

[PASTE TEXT]

4. SEO-Friendly Snippets
"Write a meta description for a webpage about [TOPIC] in under 160 characters. Make it clear, click-worthy, and non-sensational."

Legal: Risk-Free Language, Not Legal Advice

AI should never draft contracts or offer legal advice — but it can help with structuring, summarizing, and translating language into plain English.

Safe Use Cases:

- Summarizing non-sensitive policies
- Translating legal language into plain terms
- Formatting disclaimers (pre-written, not created)

Sample Prompts:

1. Legal Simplification
"Rewrite the following clause into plain English for an internal audience. Do not change its meaning or add legal advice."

[PASTE CLAUSE]

2. Structure Assistance
"List common section headers typically found in a service-level agreement (SLA) without providing legal definitions or drafting any clauses."

3. Disclaimer Formatting
"Format the following legal disclaimer for web display. Do not modify the content. Keep line spacing and readability in mind."

[PASTE DISCLAIMER]

4. Document Summary (Low Risk)
"Summarize this public-facing privacy policy in 3 bullet points for employee onboarding purposes. Avoid paraphrasing sensitive clauses."

[LINK OR TEXT]

HR: Inclusive, Professional, and Policy-Aligned

HR teams often use AI to craft onboarding documents, job postings, and culture materials — areas where tone and bias matter deeply.

Safe Use Cases:

- Job ad drafting (with inclusivity cues)
- Explaining benefits or policies in plain English
- Welcome email templates

Sample Prompts:

1. Inclusive Job Posting
"Write a job description for a [ROLE] at a small business. Use inclusive language, avoid age or gender assumptions, and focus on skills and values. Keep it under 300 words."

2. Policy Explanation
"Summarize this internal policy for new employees in an easy-to-understand tone. Keep it factual, professional, and non-legal."

[PASTE POLICY]

3. Welcome Message
"Draft a short, warm welcome email for a new team member joining the [DEPARTMENT] team. Avoid humor or personal references."

4. Performance Feedback Template
"Create a neutral, constructive performance review template for managers to use. Focus on clarity, growth mindset, and respectful tone."

Support: Empathetic, Escalation-Aware, and Brand-Protective

Support teams often turn to AI to draft replies, troubleshoot responses, and manage FAQs — but empathy and escalation logic must guide every output.

Safe Use Cases:

- Drafting first responses (for review before sending)
- Rewriting knowledge base entries
- Creating escalation handoff language

Sample Prompts:

1. Customer Reply Draft
"Write a first-response email to a customer who is reporting a [minor issue]. Keep the tone empathetic, calm, and professional. Do not offer a solution unless provided. Flag the issue for review."

2. Knowledge Base Article
"Summarize the following troubleshooting steps for [PRODUCT ISSUE] in 3 clear bullet points. Use plain language for a non-technical reader."

[STEPS]

3. Escalation Message
"Draft a response that acknowledges the customer's concern and politely informs them that their request will be escalated to a human agent. Keep it respectful and human-sounding."

4. Tone Check
"Review this drafted response for tone. Adjust it to be more empathetic and clear while keeping it under 100 words."

[PASTE RESPONSE]

Final Guidance: Safe Prompting Principles for Every Team

Regardless of role, follow these universal best practices:

Prompt Safety Do's:

- ☑ Be specific about tone, format, and audience
- ☑ Ask for assistance, not authority ("suggest" vs. "decide")
- ☑ Keep sensitive information out of prompts
- ☑ Use placeholders (e.g., [CLIENT NAME], [PRODUCT]) when drafting
- ☑ Always review AI outputs before publishing or sending

Prompt Safety Don'ts:

- ✖ Don't ask AI to interpret laws, contracts, or regulations
- ✖ Don't request final outputs without human review
- ✖ Don't treat AI as a substitute for expert judgment
- ✖ Don't include personal, financial, or proprietary data in your inputs

Conclusion

A well-structured prompt is your first — and best — defense against AI misuse. With this role-specific library, your teams can move faster while staying on-brand, compliant, and in control.

Train your staff to treat prompts like professional tools, not shortcuts. With the right habits, AI becomes a trusted collaborator — not a liability.

This is how you scale smartly, work efficiently, and protect what matters most.

End of Book
Thanks for reading. Stay sharp, stay human, and lead with intention in the age of AI.

CHECK YOUR BONUS AT THE END !

Glossary of Key AI Terms for SMB Leaders

Clear, practical definitions for busy business owners, team leads, and non-technical professionals using AI tools across their organization.

A

AI (Artificial Intelligence)
Software that simulates human thinking to analyze data, make predictions, or generate content. It can perform tasks like summarizing text, writing emails, or detecting fraud — but it lacks true understanding or judgment.

API (Application Programming Interface)
A way for software tools to talk to each other. In AI, APIs let you plug powerful AI features (like chat, image generation, or analysis) into your own apps or websites.

B

Bias (Algorithmic Bias)
When AI favors or discriminates against certain inputs, often unintentionally. This happens because the AI was trained on biased or unbalanced data. Bias can lead to unfair decisions in hiring, pricing, or support.

Bot
Short for "robot." A simple program — often using AI — that automates interactions, like answering FAQs or guiding users through a support form.

C

Chatbot
An AI tool that interacts with users through conversation. Common in customer support or on websites, but not always capable of handling complex or emotional issues.

Cloud-Based AI
AI tools that run on the internet (the cloud), not on your own devices. This makes them accessible anywhere — but means you must trust the vendor's security and data handling.

Confidence Score
A rating of how certain an AI is about its answer. Low confidence means the result is more likely to be wrong and should be reviewed by a human.

Content Generation
The use of AI to automatically write blogs, social posts, product descriptions, or emails. Often fast and useful — but needs human editing to ensure accuracy and tone.

D

Data Leakage
When private or sensitive information is accidentally exposed through AI tools — often because it was pasted into a public model or used without proper safeguards.

Deep Learning
A complex type of AI that mimics the way the human brain learns. It's behind most advanced AI tools — but behaves like a pattern matcher, not a reasoning machine.

Disclaimers (AI-Generated)
Notices you add to AI content to make clear it was machine-generated and should be reviewed before being treated as final.

E

Escalation Path (AI Support)
A rule or process that tells an AI when to stop handling a situation and pass it to a human — especially useful for complaints, billing issues, or legal matters.

Explainability
How clearly an AI can show or explain why it made a decision. Critical in high-stakes areas like hiring or finance.

F

Fine-Tuning
A method of training an AI on specific examples to make it perform better in your context — like learning your brand tone or product features. Useful, but needs expert oversight.

G

Generative AI
AI that creates something new — such as text, images, or audio — instead of just analyzing data. ChatGPT, DALL·E, and similar tools are examples.

Guardrails (AI)
Policies, prompts, or software settings that limit what AI tools can do to prevent risky, biased, or inappropriate outputs.

H

Hallucination (AI)
When AI "makes things up" — fabricating facts, quotes, sources, or references with confidence. One of the most dangerous risks in business content.

Human-in-the-Loop (HITL)
A workflow where a person reviews or approves AI output before it goes live. A key safeguard for accuracy, tone, and legal compliance.

I

Inclusion Prompting
Writing prompts that encourage diverse, fair, and bias-aware outputs from AI — especially in HR, marketing, and communications.

Incident Response (AI)
A defined plan for what to do when an AI makes a mistake — including rollback steps, communications, and review.

L

LLM (Large Language Model)
The type of AI behind tools like ChatGPT. Trained on massive amounts of text to predict and generate human-sounding language.

Logging (AI Activity)
The practice of tracking who used an AI tool, when, and for what —
critical for audit trails and accountability.

M

Model Drift
When an AI tool starts to behave differently over time — either due
to updates, new data, or system changes. Can lead to unexpected or
off-brand outputs.

Masking (Prompt Data)
Removing or replacing sensitive information in a prompt before
sending it to an AI (e.g., using [CLIENT NAME] instead of the real
name).

N

Natural Language Processing (NLP)
The field of AI focused on understanding and generating human
language. Powers chatbots, summarizers, and content tools.

NDA (Non-Disclosure Agreement)
A legal contract to protect private information. Pasting NDA-
covered info into a public AI tool can violate the agreement.

O

Output Review
The process of checking AI results for tone, accuracy, bias, or brand
alignment before publishing or using the content.

P

Prompt
The instruction or question you give to an AI tool. A good prompt leads to better, safer results. A vague prompt often produces poor or risky outputs.

Prompt Injection
A form of AI misuse where a prompt is crafted to manipulate or bypass the intended behavior of the system.

Q

Quality Assurance (QA)
The human-led step of reviewing and refining AI-generated content to ensure it meets standards, tone, and accuracy.

R

Red Teaming (AI)
Deliberate testing of AI systems to find flaws, biases, or vulnerabilities — often done by cybersecurity or compliance teams.

Rollback Plan (AI Errors)
Your emergency method for undoing AI-generated changes that go wrong — like restoring original prices or removing bad content.

S

Shadow AI
The use of AI tools by employees without formal approval or oversight — often a major visibility and security risk.

Sensitive Data
Information that should not be shared with public AI tools, such as personal names, client contracts, pricing, or legal drafts.

T

Tone Control (AI Content)
Guiding the AI to write in your brand's voice — friendly, professional, casual, etc. Often requires example prompts and post-editing.

Training Data
The information an AI learns from. If the training data is biased, outdated, or flawed, the AI's output may reflect those issues.

U

Use Policy (AI)
Your company's rules for how employees should — and should not — use AI tools. Helps reduce misuse and protect brand reputation.

V

Version Control (AI Outputs)
Tracking changes to AI-generated documents or content so you can revert back if something goes wrong.

Visibility Tools
Software that gives leadership insight into where and how AI tools are being used across the company — key for governance.

W

Workflow Automation (AI)
Using AI to streamline repetitive business tasks — like tagging emails, classifying content, or generating responses. Must include review steps for safety.

Final Note

This glossary isn't meant to make you a technical expert — it's here to make you a **confident leader in an AI-driven world**. When your team knows these terms, your policies get stronger, your decisions get smarter, and your risks get lower.

Keep it close. Update it often. Share it widely.
AI isn't replacing your team — it's reshaping how they work. Let's help them work smarter — and safer.

Bonus – FREE eBook Version

Want the full-color PDF version of this book?
Simply email me at **ericl@acrasolution.com** with a **screenshot of your Amazon purchase**, and I'll gladly send you your personal copy.

Thank you for taking the time to read this eBook.

Your support means more than you know. **By purchasing this book, you're directly contributing to the creation of more high-quality, practical resources** for business owners, IT leaders, and everyday professionals navigating the complex world of cybersecurity. It's because of readers like you that I can continue researching, writing, and delivering tools that make a real difference.

Whether you leave a positive review, recommend this book to a colleague, or simply apply what you've learned — **you're helping grow a stronger, safer business community. And for that, I sincerely thank you.**

At **AcraSolution**, we're committed to providing both premium services and a wide range of **free, actionable tools**. Our growing library includes documentation, articles, and step-by-step guides — designed to bring you immediate value, no strings attached.

If you need additional guidance or support, don't hesitate to visit our website www.acrasolution.com or reach out directly.

Together, we can build a more secure future.

— *Eric LeBouthillier*
Author & Cybersecurity Strategist

www.ingramcontent.com/pod-product-compliance
Lightning Source LLC
Chambersburg PA
CBHW071459210326
41597CB00018B/2611